ORDINARY
WORDS

The publication of this book is made possible in part by a grant from the Eric Mathieu King Fund of The Academy of American Poets.

ALSO BY RUTH STONE

Simplicity
Nursery Rhymes From Mother Stone
Who Is the Widow's Muse?
Unknown Messages
The Solution
Second-Hand Coat, Poems New and Selected
American Milk
Cheap, New Poems and Ballads
Topography and Other Poems
In an Iridescent Time

RUTH STONE

PARIS
PRESS   *Ashfield, Massachusetts 1999*

A CD of Ruth Stone reading from Ordinary Words
is also available from the Publisher.

Paris Press extends heartfelt thanks to The Academy
of American Poets, the Massachusetts Cultural
Council, the Lydia B. Stokes Foundation, and
the many individuals whose generosity made
the publication of Ordinary Words possible. We are
also indebted to the hard work and dedication
of Maryellen Ryan and Emily Cooney.

Library of Congress Cataloging-in-Publication Data
Stone, Ruth.
        Ordinary Words / by Ruth Stone. - - 1st ed.
        p. cm.
    I. Title.
    PS3537_T6817   074   1999
    811'_54 - - dc21   99-29931
                                                    CIP
ISBN 0-9638183-9-2

First Edition.

0 9 8 7 6 5 4 3 2 1

Printed in the United States of America.

For my beautiful daughters,
Marcia, Phoebe, and Abigail.

ACKNOWLEDGMENTS

I offer my gratitude to the editors of the journals
where the poems in this collection originally
appeared: The *American Voice, Boulevard, Chelsea,
Feminist Studies, Green Mountains Review, The Iowa Review,
The Kenyon Review, Lips, The Massachusetts Review, Mudfish,
North Stone Review, Passager, Painted Bride Quarterly, The
Paterson Literary Review, Ploughshares, Poetry, Prairie
Schooner,* and *Salamander.*

CONTENTS

ORDINARY
WORDS

GOOD ADVICE

Here is not exactly here
because it passed by there
two seconds ago;
where it will not come back.
Although you adjust to this—
it's nothing, you say,
just the way it is.
How poor we are,
with all this running
through our fingers.
"Here," says the Devil,
"Eat. It's Paradise."

UP THERE

Belshazzar saw this blue
as he came into the walled garden,
though outside all was yellow,
sunlight striking the fractals of sand,
the wind striating the sand in riffles.

Land changes slowly, the fathoms
overhead accruing particles,
reflecting blue or less blue.

Vapor, a transient thing; a dervish
seen rising in a whirl of wind,
or brief cloud casting its changing shadow;
though below, the open-mouthed might stand
transfixed by mirage, a visionary oasis.

Nevertheless, this deep upside-down
wash, watercolor, above planted gardens,
tended pomegranates, rouged soles of the feet
of lovers lounging in an open tent;
the hot blue above; the harem
tethered and restless as camels.

This quick vision between walls, event,
freak ball, shook jar of vapor,
all those whose eyes were not gouged out,
have looked up and seen within the cowl
this tenuous wavelength.

WORDS

Wallace Stevens says,
"A poet looks at the world
as a man looks at a woman."

I can never know what a man sees
when he looks at a woman.

That is a sealed universe.

On the outside of the bubble
everything is stretched to infinity.

Along the blacktop, trees are bearded as old men,
like rows of nodding gray-bearded mandarins.
Their secondhand beards were spun by female gypsy moths.

All mandarins are trapped in their images.

A poet looks at the world
as a woman looks at a man.

THIS

Shadow of too much knowing, days wasted in light.
Crossing some street to find diversion for a moment.
Cities scattered like a deal of cards.

On the ship hung with colored lanterns,
slipping past the island of the desperate,
we leaned looking back at what we were leaving.

It comes between the legs;
it comes out of the bag,
this sly shadow of too much knowing.

As I run on miraculous hooves
from the wooden pen. As I run
through the market street squealing.

This glaze of vision fragmented,
confetti caught in the updraft;
dark photograph of the penumbra.

THE DARK

In the dark of the moon
under the shadow of our local hydrogen fluff,
I look out of my worn eyes
and see the bright new Pleiades.
My sister lies in a box
in a New England graveyard.
By now her eyes are smears of gristle.
Her little breasts are wizened flaps.
But there, thriving in leaps and burning,
this nursery of stars, young in the universe
and yet so ancient to us.
At the start, without opticals,
they were The Seven Sisters.
We who grow old so fast
may not perceive their turbulent birth.
My darling suffered so; her cells
bursting and burning, eaten alive.
In this slow terrible way, we come to know
violent chaos at the pure brutal heart.

SUMMING IT UP

The outside is the natural enemy of the inside,
and the inside keeps pouring outside
all that the outside keeps putting inside.
"Yes," says the outside,
"I am changing. I used to be so smooth.
What are all these lumps?"
Immediately the outside opens up
and puts a five-course Chinese dinner
into the inside.
"Where am I going?" says the outside,
looking in the bathroom mirror.
Street after street, in graphs of dark intent,
move relentlessly into the fir-bearing mountains.

1941

I wore a large brim hat
like the women in the ads.
How thin I was: such skin.
Yes. It was Indianapolis;
a taste of sin.

You had a natural Afro;
no money for a haircut.
We were in the seedy part;
the buildings all run-down;
the record shop, the jazz
impeccable. We moved like
the blind, relying on our touch.
At the corner coffee shop,
after an hour's play, with our
serious game on paper,
the waitress asked us
to move on. It wasn't much.

Oh mortal love, your bones
were beautiful. I traced them
with my fingers. Now the light
grows less. You were so angular.
The air darkens with steel
and smoke. The cracked world
about to disintegrate,
in the arms of my total happiness.

HOW THEY GOT HER TO QUIET DOWN

When the ceiling plaster fell in Aunt Mabel's kitchen
out in the country (she carried her water uphill
by bucket, got all her own wood in),
that was seventy-five years ago, before she
took her ax and chopped up the furniture.
Before they sent her to the asylum.
Shafe, father of the boys (she didn't have a girl),
was running around with a loose woman.
Earlier Shafe threw the baby up against the ceiling.
"Just tossing him," he said. Little Ustie came down
with brain fever. In two days that child was dead.
Before that, however, the boys all jumped
on the bed upstairs and roughhoused so
that one night the ceiling fell in;
all lumped on the floor. The kitchen was a sight.
But those kids did not go to the poorhouse.
Grandma was elected to take them.
Mabel's sisters all said, "Ma, you take the boys."
Beauty is as beauty does. Grandma chased them
with a switch until they wore a bare path
around her last cottage. Grandma was small
and toothless, twisted her hair in a tight bun.
After she smashed the furniture, Mabel tried
to burn the house down. Years later when they
let Mabel out of the asylum, she was so light
you could lift her with one hand.
Buddy took her in and she lay on the iron bed
under a pieced quilt. "Quiet as a little bird," he said.

SO WHAT

For me the great truths are laced with hysteria.
How many Einsteins can we tolerate?
I leap into the uncertainty principle.
After so many smears you want to wash it off with a laugh.
Ha ha, you say. So what if it's a meltdown?
Last lines to poems I will write immediately.

MADISON IN THE MID-SIXTIES

Names, can you talk without their mirage?
What was his name . . . that rock star,
the one whose plane went down in the lake?
Trees talked all winter in click language.
It was a long drive from the East.
I arrived penniless;
called the Chairman.
"Find a motel," he said.
I could hear the background dinner party.
"Take a motel."
I sat in the Oldsmobile.
The Olds would later drop its front end
on the Interstate,
my mother in the backseat
and the hamster and Abigail.
University, where Roger, the graduate student,
gave me his endless poems to read, all
under the influence of Vosco Popa,
all mediocre.
The futile student protests,
napalm and the Feds.
My brains wadded like the Patchwork Girl of Oz;
maced lungs, the National Guard
lined up on either side of the main walk,
rifles cocked just above the passing heads,
a surefire canopy of death.
This montage upon which we write the message
that fails in language after language.

REPETITION

It's unbearable and yet, every day
you go to the city. The stench
of the dead mouse entrails
in the entrails of the car.
Or is it a larger thing
like a man's hand?
A rotten joke.
Maybe it's a pound of ground beef
that you forgot to take in
when you got back from the Grand Union
and the phone was ringing.
The flesh is angry and you
cannot drive away from it.
It says, "Get rid of me."
It is not insidious.
Harmless compared to industrial
pollution. But who would want
those vulnerable pink lungs
babies are born with?
On the obstacle course, the big tires
of the tractors, the tricky ruts
of mud and the slow-moving men
under yellow hard hats
and the women with stop signs;
the CAT shovel and finally,
the sad girl with long yellow hair,
holding her red flag
at the end of the line.

PERHAPS

This woman sits in the kitchen
at a plastic table playing computer chess.
She wonders what is making her happy.
Above her desk, postcards
from her daughter in New Guinea,
and a framed painting of another woman
who is also strangely happy,
for her coat is electric and has marvelous
plugs and outlets on it.
This is unusual, but on a wavelength
of pleasure perhaps only known to women.
The snow, which falls straight down, is weighted.
Its crystals are wet. Each crystal damp
as the soft crystals of flesh between a woman's
legs; as if in falling, the magnet of the earth
had promised a passionate joining, a penetration.
Although nothing is innocent and everything
comes to the body of the world already old
and used; this snow has lain over and over
in the gutters; there is this expectation of love
that lies on the old bones like a silk mask,
like a skein of ice.

ECHOES AND SHADOWS

Like a Japanese print, the willow,
closed in by chain-metal fence.
Along the gray corrugated warehouse
a stout woman rounds the corner.
Up from her bed, she has drunk her coffee,
and left the pot on the stove. She has
smoothed her warm sheets, covered
with a Kmart nonwoven coverlet.
Is a child still rolled tight in its nightmare,
who in the dark crept in to her soft side?
Never mind, she goes by, one plump
leg after another. Below the window
the still eye of a prowl car stares up
blank. The fresh sky paling already
with traffic fumes. In the night, planes
come in low over the roof, violent as storms;
their Doppler rise shaking our bodies.
In our dreams we attend the long fall,
the long fade of their passing flight.
In this light lifting they now pass high
in the deep background of the upper air.
Starlings walk around on the beaten
yard of the playground, they walk
around the dry fountain, and hiss
in their soft pecking order, under the fingers,
under the gray hair of the willow.

EARTHQUAKE

The moon rises as Shizu rises from her couch,
still in the shadow of her husband
who puts her to work early at his vegetable stand.
The mountains take the light.
Her calligraphy, the dark brush stroke
with which she frees herself,
lies in loose sheets on her drawing table.
The tide recedes, the tectonic plates
grind into the flesh of the peninsula.
She is one grain of sand
in the rippling ground swell;
a fan opening and closing.

MALE GORILLAS

At the doughnut shop
twenty-three silver backs
are lined up at the bar,
sitting on the stools.
It's morning coffee and trash day.
The waitress has a heavy feeling face,
considerate with carmine lipstick.
She doesn't brown my fries.
I have to stand at the counter
and insist on my order.
I take my cup of coffee to a small
inoffensive table along the wall.
At the counter the male chorus line
is lined up tight.
I look at their almost identical butts,
their buddy hunched shoulders,
the curve of their ancient spines.
They are methodically browsing
in their own territory.
This data goes into that vast
confused library, the female mind.

NEVER

Don't forget that Henry James,
because he was afraid
of his hostility toward women
and his sentimental attachment to men,
spread his impotence into language.
He went on and on and couldn't cum.

His style differed from Proust's.
Proust delayed the sensual,
dragging the orgasm out for pages,
until the entire skin of the body
was tortured with pleasure.

But he came, yes, by transvestite
or by tea and cake. The disrobing
went on slowly over and over;
the sensual countryside,
the ridiculous fag, the elegant taster,
the style; coarse broad breast,
kitchen and ballroom, spite
and desperate addiction; climax,
always long drawn-out climax
that only one lying for years
remembering could make
every moment into an hour,
the immortal flesh.

AN EDUCATION IN THE EIGHTIES

I'm in the Grandparent's Program
at the Happyvale School.
It ekes out the S.S.
This morning I pass a child,
elbows up like wings, his hands
in breast-high leather pockets. He's
headed down the mountain, but not to school.
He don't go to school. Up here on the mountain
them two women and seven children
share the same man.
He comes in from wherever,
conspicuous in that getup;
decides which beast to slaughter.
Always a gaggle of geese out on the highway.
On the back road,
all of a sudden he'll show,
straddle a poorly fed horse.
Their big old ram, sweetbreads hanging like an extra leg,
goes blatting ahead of my Buick.
Their barn door hangs on one hinge.
Built seven years ago by an out-of-stater
who married a second time after his wife
ran off. Married one of the Jones
girls, the mean one who used to tie
the step-daughter to the end of the bed
where she would scream for hours.
He built that barn and house out of green wood,
and when it dried it buckled.
It buckled after he sold it for spite to them folks
in a fracas over his local taxes.
They serve a hot lunch at school
and we senior citizens get the same menu

as the fourth graders. It's all measured out
just so, none left over. You take what's flobbed
on the plate and stay in line
even if you wet your pants.

ABSENCE PROVES NOTHING

By noon I can't stop writing.
I'm on the back of last night,
a reverse gallop.
Last night I lay turning—asking—
what is the telephone pole good for
if not the woodbine?
Because of men, women translate fear.
Thus, all women present subliminally.
That the killer did not come last night
proves nothing.
At night, what is a glass window?
Only a dark space reflecting yourself.
Only a lens for the one outside.

SO WHAT'S WRONG?

Here it is, a green world
and all of these millions
living in the dust.
It's like a dog with a chain
that's just as long as this worn
path around the post.
How the dog loves the hand
that brings it water;
the voice up there,
almost out of reach, that says,
"Here is your food.
Nice dog."
While it eats, like a dream,
the voice goes away;
and there is the path
around the post.
Joyful dog, something,
somewhere, is so wonderful.
And at night, the dog
lies down and its muscles
remember the ferns,
the hot smell of the field
sloping downhill,
the clouds breaking,
and that light,
like mist, like smoke;
the strange reflected light
of a dead moon.

RELATIVES

Grandma lives in this town;
in fact all over this town.
Grandpa's dead.
Uncle Heery's brain-dead,
and them aunts! Well!
It's grandma you have to contend with.
She's here—she's there!
She works in the fast-food hangout.
She's doing school lunches.
She's the crossing guard at the school corner.
She's the librarian's assistant.
She's part-time in the real-estate office.
She's stuffing envelopes.
She gets up at three a.m.
to go to the screw factory;
and at night she's at the business school
taking a course in computer science.

Now you take this next town.
Grandpa's laid out neat in the cemetery
and grandma's gone wild and bought a bus ticket
to Disneyland.
Uncle Bimbo's been laid up for ten years
and them aunts
are all cashiers in ladies' clothing
and grandma couldn't stand the sight of them
washing their hands and their hair
and their panty hose.
"It's Marine World for me," grandma says.

STRANDS

This uprooted grass from the edge of the marsh-lake
is green and beginning to rot,
so that some strands are brown as Hillery's hair,
and fine and bleached as Bianca's hair.
A small snail is passenger at the tip of one strand.
But it does not seem to move.
It is fastened. A bird could use this grass.
As it lies over my left hand, drying in the air,
at the finial point a protrusion of bud-knobs,
like flowers in small cylinders.
It is almost the skeleton of itself as it dries.
On my palm it could be the threads
for stitching something together.
These grasses, silent as ourselves
as we went about making ourselves
from our mothers' bodies, as they grew
up through the shallows to the surface,
where I look down at my bird body.
The mother, the wind moving over the surface;
the mother holding the roots in the silty bottom.
Now the sister can begin to weave
the body of the shirts for the six swan brothers.
The brothers move over the lake,
looking down at their bird bodies.
This marsh grass could be like my mother's fingers
in the garden. The green and brown stains of grass
on her fingers in the garden.
And this light grass on my hand
is like her hair, light and sweet smelling,
now as hay drying in the sun is sweet smelling.
The snail among the strands like myself, clinging.

CAN CRANES COGITATE?

All alone a young crane stood on a sand hill.
Father, he cried, I am lonely. Give me an egg.
Son, the father said, smiling ever so slightly,
you are getting ahead of yourself. Eggs are not
that easy to come by. The mysterious egg
is a process unto itself. Even I am not sure
how this miracle occurs. I am loath to admit
that my wife, who certainly was not known
for her brain, seemed to have an occult power
when it came to eggs. She sat on them, you know.
The young crane immediately found a gaggle
of swans' eggs. That's simple, he said. And sat down.
When the irate swans arrived, they bit and battered
the badly mistaken crane. Thief, murderer, they hissed.
But I want to be a father, cried the ignorant crane.
Birds of a feather flock together, the mother swan
hinted, albeit in a nasty tone of voice. The father swan
coughed and looked aside. Get thee to a nunnery, son,
he advised. Confidentially, son, that's from an old roué.

AESTHETICS OF THE CATTLE FARM

Every day I walked to the pond;
dry cracked soil, sparse pasture;
the surface of the pond like quick silver.
Then, following a path
over blue chicory-dotted stubble
to bristled weeds and copse,
to a cemetery of bleached bones.
A few upright black feathers,
quills struck in the stiff mud;
the soft glow of hidden things
sculptured by weather.
A small funereal woods
into which the farmer dragged
the diseased cattle and left
them to fall to their knees.
Attending buzzards
came to pick the flesh;
the large separated vertebrae
scattered in the coarse undergrowth;
exquisite segments, fluted
and glistening like angel wings.

INCREDIBLE BUYS IN

Houston, fourth largest city in the country.
"I dunno," says the man across the aisle,
trimmed beard, cowboy hat, designer jeans.
From the train we see a line of Black Angus,
mothers and calves, crossing an endless field.
"Can't say," he says, "where anything is.
Only been assigned down here five months."

Wherever you are, I think to my absent friends,
the ones I am leaving behind in Houston,
if you're working out in a glass building
with neon lights, air stinging your nose
and eyes, chlorine; the tight bright blues
and reds stretch-slick over your thighs
and buttocks, treading the pressure stairs,
lifting the weights: you know you're keeping fit.

Well, my eyes are blind to what I missed.
Can't think of it. Transported cultures,
exotic fragile crafts. Those price tags with
hidden messages. Someone's blood for your
cash, someone's breath; hand painted, hand
sewn, hand carved. I know, far away the maker,
the sweat-laborer, is lying down; her long
black hair loosened, her plump lips parted,
the terrors flickering behind smooth eyelids;
someone's taut naked body that she strokes
with her small capable hands, lying beside her,
sleeping in the same stone garden,
deep in the soft ooze of my cortex.

LIGHT CONCLUSIONS

Seven light bulbs burned for seven hours.
Delicate but well made,
their seven eyes stared at the leather-hooded killer.
He moved with the wind outside the black window.
Eventually everyone fell asleep.
The bulbs, hissing and trembling, sent tender ohms
over the strange lonely woman.
"What sentiment!" they observed,
as they jiggled their fine tongues crafted in Hong Kong.

UNCLE CAL ON FASHIONS

Troy, New York! Where they made celluloid collars!
Great center for celluloid collars!
Someone might say, "His collar exploded!"
You mean he got hot under the collar?
"Went up like wax! Flammable stuff, celluloid collars!"
Didn't take much to ignite, but they were stiff.
They could hold up your chin. Several chins.
I've seen men resting on them.
But the cigar ash, it posed a certain risk.
Of course in the privacy of the bedroom, you'd take them off.
It was nothing at a large dinner party to see several exploding.
Of course, it would be after the ladies withdrew.
And if you had a beard—well, it was quite a flash.
This was fine for the tablecloth business.
Table linens moved fast in those days.
But some ladies took exception to the loss of linens,
heirlooms and so forth. Got so an invitation
to dinner might say "RSVP and SCC"—
sans celluloid collar, you know.
The less bold ones might say, "soft collar requested."
Yep. Some mighty red necks.
Yep. Back then Troy was like a plug of dynamite
with a short fuse. That's where the expression
"he's a turkey" came from. Then some feller invented starch.
But 'twasn't the same.

YES, THINK

Mother, said a small tomato caterpillar to a wasp,
why are you kissing me so hard on my back?
You'll see, said the industrious wasp, deftly inserting
a package of her eggs under the small caterpillar's skin.
Every day the small caterpillar ate and ate the delicious
tomato leaves. I am surely getting larger, it said to itself.
This was a sad miscalculation. The ravenous hatched
wasp worms were getting larger. Oh world, the small
caterpillar said, you were so beautiful. I am only a small
tomato caterpillar, made to eat the good tomato leaves.
Now I am so tired. And I am getting even smaller. Nature
smiled. Never mind, dear, she said. You are a lovely link
in the great chain of being. Think how lucky it is to be born.

HUMMINGBIRDS

Driving the perfect fuel, their thermonuclear wings,
into the hot layer of the sugar's chromosphere,
hummingbirds in Egypt
might have visited the tombs of the Pharaohs
when they were fresh in their oils and perfumes.
The pyramids fitted,
stone slab against slab,
with little breathers, narrow slits of light,
where a few esters, a sweet resinous wind,
might have risen soft as a parachute.
Robbers breached the false doors,
the trick halls often booby traps,
embalming them in the powder of crushed rock.
These, too, they might have visited.
The miniature dagger hangs in the air,
entering the wild furnace of the flower's heart.

THE WAYS OF DAUGHTERS

My daughters are getting on.
They're in over their hips,
over their stretch marks.
Their debts are rising
and their faces are serious.

There are no great barns
or riding horses.
Only one of them has a washing machine.
Their old cars break
and are never fixed.

So what is this substance
that floods over them,
into which they wade
as if going out
to meet the Phoenicians?

And they have no nets
for those shifty-looking sailors.
But when I look again,
my daughters are alone in their kitchens.
Each child sweats in its junior bed.

And my girls are painting their fingernails.
They're rubbing lotions
on their impatient hands. This year
they are staining their hands and feet with henna.
They lie in the sun with henna packs on their hair.

THEN

That summer, from the back porch,
we would hear the storm like a train,
the Doppler effect compressing the air;
the rain, a heavy machine, coming up
from below the orchard, rushing toward us.
My trouble was I could not keep you dead.
You entered even the inanimate,
returning in endless guises.
And that winter an ermine moved into the house.
It was so cold the beams cracked.
The ermine's fur was creamy white
with the last half of the tail soot black.
Its body about ten inches long,
it slipped through small holes.
It watched us from a high shelf in the kitchen.
In our loss we accepted the strange shape of things
as though it had a meaning for us,
as though we moved slowly over the acreage,
as though the ground modulated like water.
The floors and the cupboards slanted to the West,
the house sinking toward the evening side of the sky.
The children and I sitting together waiting,
there on the back porch, the massive engine
of the storm swelling up through the undergrowth,
pounding toward us.

ORDINARY WORDS

Once I called you a dirty—whatever.
Now it does not matter
because your clothes have become
a bundle of rags.
Then I wanted to see what it felt like.
I paid with my life for that.
It went behind your skull.
My middle-class beauty, testing itself,
discovered the dull dregs of ordinary marriage.
Thick lackluster spread between our legs.
We used the poor lovers to death.

Like an ancient reed,
three notes in the early morning,
in the mountains
where I have never traveled,
the blind bird remembers its sorrow.

WHEN

When you return, iron maiden,
jaws of despair,
the thrifty will have eaten the fat.
I, too, have lived on her; the old woman.

When the house is empty,
those outside stare in;
only the flapping door.
Iron maiden, cruel jaws of despair,

when you return, her face will be like that;
the door to the cellar standing open.
When you show your mouth of nails,
only the wind's body will be there.

PATIENCE

You hacked the firewood out of the stiffened snow.
Winter demands a vital patience.
Driven inside this narrow space,
now you are splitting illusions. In the disordered room,
the stove heats up, the temperature rises.
Outside, wind soughs through a nursery of trees.
The trees, their white roots aching under ice,
tubes of patience; cork, cambium, chains of cells
twisting, looping up stairways, terminal tunnels.
Patient as the coral snake in the double sleeping bag
with the newlyweds on their first night in the desert,
with them inside their zipped bed.
You read about them before you burned the paper.
The coral snake, its small mouth, patiently,
automatically, trapped in that cloth of strangeness,
working the venom into their flesh.
Days later, when the police unzipped the bag
to pull the bodies out, the coral snake was still there.
As similar as one tree creaking against another,
these blunders of atoms, these circumstantial crimes.
While fixing your dinner, you thought about those
newlyweds, hoping they died after their orgasm,
or at its peak—that cosmic rush to the very edge,
to the nothing that is. In itself, the orgasm,
phenomenon of blunders and patient violence,
always comes with a little touch of death.

ONE THOUGHT

Accompanied
by many pictures,
the words
swelled and shrank.
The brain
flashed intermittently,
easily explained
in a simple collider.
The energy of nothing
smashed into the
energy of something.
There was complicity
in our smiles.
One thought—
I cannot live without you,
oh brief and inconceivable other.

RESIDUE

Will I ever feel again?
Living at loose ends,
nothing finished.
The odor of your body
sometimes returns
in the afternoon.
A déjà vu rises from
books in the back room,
poems of Wallace Stevens;
your Fruit of the Loom shorts
packed so long in the attic,
alternately freezing and thawing;
or the picture of Delmore Schwartz
sitting on a bench
in a small fenced-in park;
his long gangster-style coat,
his legs crossed;
the edges of a newspaper
lifting in the wind;
his vacant stare, dead white,
vaguely petulant, lost.
Trying to remember you,
I ask myself, who
was that dark Semite?
Your face, your voice,
all but your hands
and feet, faded.

SORTING IT OUT

Falsely soft, infinitely far,
the chlorophyll machine.
Each socket knocked by a photon
from the mother star.

It's the trees and their green flesh.
Listen, our fingers feel the hiss.
The great blue whale
picks up the sonar.

This obsession with invisible things.

But the concrete with its gray crumbling smile
is like a factual male.
Drive your car into me, it suggests:
I'm no bloody vagina.

The concrete stretches for miles;
the turrets with guns in position.

THE TRADE-OFF

Words make the thoughts.
Severe tyrants, like the scrubbers
and guardians of your cells.
They herd your visions
down the ramp to nexus,
waiting with sledgehammers
to knock what is the knowing
without knowing into knowledge.
Yes, the tight bag of grammar,
syntax, the clever sidestep
from babble, is a comfortable
prison. A mirror of the mirror.
And all that is uttered in its chains
is locked out from the secret.

ROMANCE

I went back, as to my relatives.
When I arrived, the elms had been shaved.
But you were all the same.
The buildings, the dry classrooms.
I embraced your eyes, your avenues.
You were fixed in the same expressions.
Your flat voices, your dental work,
like your lips, slipping over words already said.
Additional agricultural pamphlets;
many of you sat in private offices.
Why did I think I could drag it all back,
the former edge of town where
streets ended in fields under clouds
puffed like the French phrases
he kissed me with in the sucked-in breath
of that illusive happiness.
Coming back, listening, looking;
ready to take your bodies in my hands.
Returning to streets that had poured
heavy shopping malls
over the hay-sweet grass
where he and I lay whispering
the most important nonsense
of my desperate and embittered life.

READING

It is spring when the storks return.
They rise from storied roofs.
In the quick winter afternoon
you lie on your bed
with a library book close to your face,
your body on a single bed,
and the storks rise
with the sound of a lifted sash.
You know without looking
that a servant girl
is leaning out in the soft foreign air.
A slow spiral of smoke
from green firewood
is reflected in her eyes.
She moves down an outside stair
absently driving the poultry.
The storks are standing on the roof.
The girl wraps her hands in her apron.
Small yellow flowers
have clumped among the tussocks
of coarse grass.
She listens with her mouth open
to something you cannot hear.
Your body is asleep.
She smiles.
She does not know a cavalry is coming
on a mud rutted road,
and men with minds like ferrets
are stamping their heavy boots
along the pages.

WITH LOVE

You sent narcissus bulbs.
They stretch up in the window,
their long necks like geese,
out of the fat cluster.
The feathers of pine trees
crusted with last night's feathery fall.

Longing to go north
where what survives
curls under the drifts.

Not so sure of the voice,
the cavern slowly uninhabited.
The ermine still poised
on the upper shelf,
carefully listening.

What is continuous is mirage.
Here I am opening my eyes again.
What? Is it still winter?

Here he sat and told me these slight
terrible traumas of his.

The peculiar gushers of light,
the behavior of plasma and gas in nova;
the rolling tides, the waves
on the Outer Banks, similar;
and yet for every one of us,
four pounds of pesticide. Not so bad,
says the U.S. Department of Agriculture.
Only four pounds a year for each of us.
When you swallow it down, you will hardly notice.

SO BE IT

Look, this string of words
is coming out of my mouth,
or was. Now it's coming
out of this pen whose ink
came from Chattanooga.
Something tells me
Chattanooga was a chief.
He came out of his mother's
body. He pushed down
the long tube that got
tighter and tighter until
he split it open and stuck
his head out into a cold
hollow. Holding his belly
by a bloody string he
screamed, "I am me,"
and became a cursive
mark on a notepad that
was a former tree taken
with other trees in the
midst of life and mutilated
beyond all remembrance
of the struggle from seed
to cambium; the slow
dying roots feeling for some
meaning in the eroded
soil; the stench of decay
sucked into the chitin
of scavengers, becoming
alien to xylem and phloem,
the vast vertical system
of reaching up. For there

is nothing that is nothing,
but always becoming
something; flinging itself;
leaping from level to level.

IN THE ARBORETUM

Near the path where I am casually walking, in sight of the main
building, where at night from my gratuitous rooms I physically
flinch when the great-horned owl goes soft as dust across
the clearing, his cry piercing my mask as he settles his claws
around a branch that juts out from the oak nearest my balcony,
and like the seasoned woodwind player in a three-piece combo
plays to a woman sitting at a special table with her friends, lets us
have it, his great riffs coming right from his gonads. The entire
preserve knows this is his territory. And near the path, a fledgling
hawk is down, motionless in the leaves. It is afternoon, and
autumn in California in the redwoods, not the great redwoods of
the north, but relatively young redwoods already tall enough and
too closely spaced, like saplings still fighting it out for the light.
I am walking casually in sight of my artist-in-residence rooms on
the second floor, fulfilling the letter of a will left by a rich man
in memory of his wife who wrote novels. No one remembers
them but I look at her portrait every day as I walk out my door.
I remember her. She is my benefactor. These were their rooms,
their grounds, their fake Greek sculpture and their too loosely
interpreted will. The mansion and gardens have been taken
over by friends of the trustees who make it pay for its upkeep
with blatant commercial ventures. Weddings take place here.
Models are photographed here. Troops of scouts picnic on the
great lawns and defy gravity on the steep cliffs. The fledgling
hawk, still as a stone god, every feather hunched between
scapulars, is down on the mottled ground just off the path
and probably has not yet learned to fly. This may be its virgin
flight and the most dangerous. It is hunched in a compact
parabola shape, mottled like the dry leaves, mimicking artifact.
Totally vulnerable, with its terrible innocence, it cannot feed
itself. It cannot fly yet. It has this brief corridor to cross. That is
what I think as I walk softly past. A half mile through the woods

where I am taking my daily walk, I see what might be the mother
perched on a bare branch, stretched up, her profile in full view.
In Vermont last year, when an eight-year-old girl disappeared,
her whole community, most of them on welfare, living in trailers,
got out and beat the fields in rows, with sticks, covering entire
corn fields, the ground around for acres, until they found her
body, her scarf knotted around her throat, her raped blood already
dried; but there she was. I return, slowly, bringing back a few
eucalyptus leaves in my pocket. I like to sniff their resinous oil.
On a clear afternoon the sky lifts farther out, its skin inflated,
as if the jets, dark arrows trailed by long white messages from
the military, were fixing the bone ribs for our shelter on the great
ice slopes. I search near the path for the hawk child. It is gone.

OVERNIGHT GUEST

Waiting for your ride in front of the house
where you spent the night,
where, as a third ear
during their endless intimate,
important, and kinky phone calls,
you pretended to rinse glassware;
you were a dog from the pound,
grateful, sniffing the upholstery.

Later, lying in the center of their
king-sized bed, a giant wall-to-wall
mirror, isolating you like a rabbit;
it was also their exercise
room with torture equipment;
something in you twitched,
flickering a bizarre video in your head.

It's morning now. You're standing
outside, with nightgown and toothbrush
wrapped in your purse, waiting for a bus
to take you somewhere else. You're depressed.
They're asleep of course. Their network wrapped
around them. You keep wondering why you're
missing something. Then you look back and see
your pricked-up ears, your waggy self, stuck
inside their picture window, where for years
it will wave at you—naive, apologetic, embarrassed.

ALL IN TIME

Behind the glass door of the waiting room,
one hundred and fifty passive-aggressive
passengers girded up for Galveston.
The bearded conductor lets them out
one by one to the named coaches.
A mother who says to her baby,
"Now you lie there until I tell you to move."
And four small girls, hair in tight cornrows,
quietly smiling at something you can't see.
An old sixties-type hippie father
is on the bench with you. He's going
off to Boise to say good-bye to his daughter
who is on her way to a Peace Corps
medical team. He has ten minutes to catch
his train in Chicago. He shows you her picture.
"One tribe," he says, "so they don't have
any wars. Flat and grassy," he says,
"just the beginnings of mountains.
Twenty-six months," he says. "That's
a long time, you know." And then the friend
you haven't seen for seven years until
this visit, the friend who seems to have emerged
like a cicada, shrill and predestined,
gets there with the coffee and carries
your heavy cases onto the train.
You both cry. She has begun to think you are
her mother and you have retreated
into your wounded child. When you say good-bye,
you pull apart like Velcro.

SCHMALTZ

Those rented rooms,
borrowed beds,
when I would lie down
with my length slack against yours
and feel those simple wounds
of the surfaces
with no thought of the garrote.
And here, after all these years,
I am still thinking
if only one more time,
that ordinary naked touch,
unconscious of its death.
And then, this morning,
the shock of an old song,
after the usual trash of the news;
schmaltz, from the big-band days;
and Sinatra, of course,
on a scratched record,
the local radio's nostalgia.
It is brief, but for a moment
my body shakes
with the remembered tremor
of your voice.
And then, the aftershock:
that he could bring it back—
this grief for which there is no cure.

THE TRINITY

The mother listens to the dreams of the daughter.
The seaweed lifts with the wave. A man
inside the green wave, the drowned man lifts up,
anchored by the long tough root.

She taught her never to say no to her desires.
The full streams of water in the mountain, the streams
of blood in the body; far as the moon, farther, glistening.
The face of the daughter glistens.

The beads of sweat, the soft hairs of the face lift and ripple,
the rising and falling breasts, the patient self, the wayward other,
rising up, the pull of the pulse;
the pale nipple of the moon calling the daughter.

The daughter lives on the outside of a dream.
The center weaves itself a riddle. The mother
listens under the water reaching for the root;
the deep flaking down of delicate bodies.

Cleaving its way pathless, pulled always in a curve,
through and around, trusting the gravity of the mother,
the small candle in the dark. The mother,
rushing toward the dark love who is always beyond her.

A MOMENT

Across the highway a heron stands
in the flooded field. It stands
as if lost in thought, on one leg, careless,
as if the field belongs to herons.
The air is clear and quiet.
Snowmelt on this second fair day.
Mother and daughter,
we sit in the parking lot
with doughnuts and coffee.
We are silent.
For a moment the wall between us
opens to the universe,
then closes.
And you go on saying
you do not want to repeat my life.

VENTRILOQUIST

This other woman in my body,
my body that has forgotten me,
not even the used bed
from the Salvation Army saves her.

The small dummies
dressed, vocalized,
performing on her knee;
the sacks of their empty
bodies stuffed in her pockets.

And if she'd lie down in the snow,
that angel would be a stranger,
but a likable fool; just gullible.
It's her incurable lust.

We're all the same;
looking for a fix, a touch,
the real silk.

Although it's true I don't pursue
any other dead body;
only yours, my poor
handful of dust.

THIS SPACE

Rushing past us
faster than this
with a few glitches,

everything you love,
like a film
in reverse.

Can this fist
in your skull
hold all that?

Like the leaves of
gloxinia, lobed maps
you cannot read,

their mysterious
patterns; fingerprints
of the universe.

Though you call it
longing, it is
the same need

that clings
in the tidal pool,
that sucks

itself to this rock
within the irresistible vector
of the ocean's pull.

UNSPEAKABLE

When Gus sees his father,
they don't speak of it.
His mother is dead.
What was it that he did
when he was ten?
He remembers his father
stripping him and hosing
him down outside,
and beating him
with a peeled switch.
Sent to his room without dinner,
he grew up dreading
the evening meal. And yet
he bought his father's
little store of stoves
and he features sets
of cooking pots.
He has every utensil necessary
and fixes himself elegant food
but then, if you are his guest,
he serves very small portions
and hustles it away saying,
"Oh, you should see the dessert."
He advertises over the local radio;
his stove shop, cast-iron stoves,
the warmth of home, the real home
where you can draw near
touching one another's feet and hands;
leaning back in your chairs,
everywhere familiar,
creating your own past.

VERMONT NATURE

George Jones, our barrel-chested hard drinking plumber,
always talked about bear hunting on the mountain.
He was on the lookout for bear all summer. "Bear season,"
he would say, "Can't fix that water pipe, ma'am."
Neighbor, Franny, sitting on our porch one evening
whispered, "Hear that?" We wouldn't have noticed
anything but Franny put hands to mouth and grunted
through his fingers. "That's bear," he said. Mixed
with the shush of leaves, an answering grunt.
"Coax them right up to you," Franny said, "this side
of the wind. Five-hundred pounds; shy.
Come down for the apples."

My sister lived farther up in the woods.
A bear passed over her land in plain sight.
She watched it travel through trees from beaver dam
to birches, across her slope. It was a big bear,
didn't make any noise. She never saw another
but always had that hope and kept binoculars ready;
put up a sign, BEAR CROSSING, but then got worried
about whether George would notice and take advantage
of the fact. So she put the sign up over her bed.

PREFAB

Following this white prefab
lumbering on the highway;
we are passed by
the gloved and leather-capped
driver of a red Porsche,
who gives us the finger.
We return the compliment.
We are dazy with heat,
and somehow, the idea of houses
moving in the air above the trees
seems implicit, or ourselves,
like helium balloons, following
in the guise of mechanical angels.

Complete in themselves,
the houses, long boxes ready
to reassemble your life
whenever the truck cab pulls in
and backs up, often after dark,
where the two-lane road
splits the farmland,
where the miserable young steers
are standing in muddy pens.
Red lanterns hold back the pickups,
and teenagers in revved up Chryslers
sit in line, lighting up the dark road,
while the curious house-raising,
now in its instant package,
like a cylinder of biscuit dough,
pops into place.
In the morning, the miracle:
luxurious with its kitchen,

its bath, its cupboards, its laundry,
its king-size bed.

As if the hustling contractor had rubbed
an old lamp, and an ambulant genie
had set down the palace
for this prince and this princess.

I MEET THEM

Your regular people range over
the country. It is they who visit
Yosemite and Glacier,
who retire to forty acres
in Lower-Upper Michigan
after twenty-five years
on the police force in Detroit.
They feed bears in their
backyards. They see the doe
lift her leg and swat the fawn
to the ground because it
wandered off. They see
the chastised fawn get up
and follow its mother.
Your regular people read
magazines illustrated with
winged angels. If they
are women, they work two
days a week at the beauty
parlor. They think they might
take a summer job at a National
Park. When they shoot an elk
high in the western mountains
it's toward evening so they
leave it and go down and when
they climb back up to get it
next day, a grizzly has torn
it apart and chewed it up.
All they can rescue are the antlers.

AT MCDONALD'S IN RUTLAND

I listen to two men in the next booth.
They are different from the others in here.
They are wearing lurid green and hard blue serge suits.
One says, "See, your piece of cake
might be garbage to me—like my wife says."
They are Italian-Americans.
They box each other lightly.
They rub their faces with their fingers,
feeling their fresh shaven jaws for dark stubble.
They have white teeth.
They wave their hands as they talk.
To them everything is a dramatic story.
They attract attention.
I count out my change in dimes:
one coffee and two hamburgers.
One I am saving for you.
How did I get here so poor?
Sometimes desperate, soot under my fingernails,
the wood fire burning back on the mountain
slowly depositing creosote in the chimney;
I can smell it for miles, it is in my lungs.
I come here to be near people,
to sit in McDonald's. Back in the kitchen
behind the counter, a warning signal
beeps in one tone over and over.
It reminds me of a bad TV series
where a man is always trying to escape
and he is always being brutally chased,
brutally caught and brutally dragged back
to the sinister private hospital for the insane.
Sometimes looking at all the people
in tan and brown and rust jackets

with blond and brown and blond and brown hair—
but one of the men in the booth has gray hair.
It lies in marcelled waves. In the twenties
he would have been a sheik.
Sometimes looking at all the people who don't
notice, they just drive up and get out of their cars
and come in. It's so easy to stand in line.
It's so easy to line up at the counter.
Habit, pattern, sleepwalking like barnacles
that thought they were going somewhere
without knowing that they were growing
into barnacles. Sometimes to get away
from the monotony, to be among people,
I come in here, to Rutland, to McDonald's.

THE WORD THOUGH AS A COUPLER

Though is a thick syllable,
a qualifier, a gate slowly opening;
and can be rimmed with replaceable
shark's teeth. Or tongued *although*,
may dance, bursting into esters,
geometric pollen or the chaos
of successful flowers. *Though* as one
and one may lead to love, hate,
or indifference. *Although* can never
quite spit these crucifying nails
and often flutters, exhausted
as snow-pitted vireos; those last
late clutches that survived the up-north
summer, only to be sleeted
on their flyways against the steel
lines of communication towers.

ETC.

This borrowed pressed-wood table
is molecularly unhooked in parceled impulses,
stored in my lobes where Adolph Hitler
is also shredded, his repulsive
mustache distributed throughout
my eclectic electrical system.
But that's not all.
His hoarse disembodied voice,
without a decibel, still shouts,
goose-stepping through my cracked
cranium. As now, another snowfall
sculptures an unreality, clean and fresh,
bringing down in its light crystals
industrial particulates as it settles.
Out there, a miracle;
in here, disassembled,
encoded visually, linguistically,
tagged with the rest of the garbage
that my brain recycles, that is myself;
this cumulative trash that goes with me.

SITCOM ON THE GREYHOUND
IN RUTLAND, VERMONT

Outside the stopped bus
two couples are not just kissing,
they are dry fucking.
The boy with the permed curls
has his hands under her blouse.
Her face against his left shoulder
is hidden. She presses into his
shirt. The customers on the bus
think it's the usual video. Finally
she turns toward us and we see
she is a plain fat clone wearing
glasses. Maybe she is his mother.
It's so up front these days.
The driver slams the luggage panels.
The curly-haired lover gets on.
He has grown much shorter.
He gives us the naked greaser smirk.
She crosses the street to the parking
lot as if to take a shower.
Now the other couple uncouples;
a pair of garden snakes,
they uncoil and slither apart.
She comes on board with her
tongue flickering, and the chubby
newly hired bus driver, full
of the joy of job and stand-up
comedy, gets on the mike
with his captive audience, who
are to be fertilized forever
with his monologue and privy
to his heroics with the Nurse's

Aide in sneakers and white
headband who sits right
up front egging him on.

ON THE STREET

Each day you pass this woman
sitting on the sidewalk.
She is pressed against the building.
She is wrapped as for a funeral pyre,
shawls wound around her.
Only her face looks out of this cowl
and her hands, ready to turn palms up,
if you are not hardened to her.
If you allow yourself to look closer,
you see her, as though adjusting
a microscope. Her skin comes into focus.
It is layered like fallen leaves,
blue around the lips and blotched
with ocher and brown.
The flume of the avenue sweeps
as in a monsoon, a patterned commerce
of debris. If you hesitate,
you are sucked into a chalice
of saints and miracles; the body's
unexpected lush response
to all you have hidden from yourself.

AT THE MUSEUM, 1938

In the native-bird exhibit, the whippoorwill,
stuffed with sawdust and arsenic,
hides among arranged dried leaves
in order to instruct you.
Nearby, a Navajo rug: the design
a complex ideograph, a sacred message,
a man-spirit in mirror image.
However, it is without annotation,
the legend meaningless, reduced to artifact.
Now I am looking at a photograph:
Kill Spotted Horses' ceremonial face
in a cheap frame. In a matching frame, Blue Wing,
her dark eyes set toward the mountains.
Ropes of significant beads hang from her.
Gently the round cheeks turn away.
On the winding stairs, the old oak railing
was crafted into ornate spools.
Every newel post is carved. And here,
in a glass case, as if in a logical progression,
is the tiny skeleton of a kiwi.
Outside, the great elms along the streets in Urbana,
their green arched cathedral canopies; the continuous
singing of birds among their breathing branches.

SPECULATION

A girl we didn't actually know
won a contest we never heard of
and fifty pairs of new shoes.
We each had one pair of shoes
and two skirts and two blouses.
We were in high school, my sister and I.
We washed and ironed our clothes
at night. There was a Depression.
The girl with all this footwear
sat in the Marott Hotel lobby.
She was part of a display.
It was probably some desperate
advertisement by some failing
business. We heard she was scared,
sat there without making a sound.
Her picture was in the newspaper;
Indianapolis, 1930.
My little sister and I discussed it.
We could just see her closet
with those shoes hanging
in shoe pockets. "Maybe she
shares them with her sister,"
I said to my sister, my now dead
sister. "I doubt she wears them
through." My sister and I cut
cardboard to fit inside ours
when the soles grew thin.
She said, "Maybe they're stacked
in boxes. Fifty pairs, all the right
size and all she has to do
is sit around and be seen."
We didn't exactly connect this

to Blue Beard's locked room,
but each clue, like the fatal key,
has a predecessor. My sister
died of cancer from cigarettes.
She said, with her wig on the night-
stand beside her bed, that smoking
always made her feel glamorous.

BOTTLED WATER

These plastic bottles of air in the bushel basket
were formerly filled with corporate spring water.
The water poured through my kidneys
and down the t-bowl into the sewage plant.
The bottles came from a bottling works.
Schlup, schlap, they swelled with the pressure.
Grip-top-snap; in twos on a roller,
they went to do their duty.
They had a past. They were brought forth
in batches of plastic syrup.
Their poisons rose to circle the planet.
Their labels were stamped
from the living limbs of trees.
The trees' roots suffered.
The anaerobic bacteria seethed and fermented.
In my place, I am only a sick woman,
but I have tasted Eden and it is bitter.

WESTERN PURDAH, INC.

Panty hose;
lotus-foot of the West,
iron maiden of her sex,
pseudo chastity belt.

On a clothesline they present
the lower half of her
that kicks and screams in mime.
These are the blood constrictors.
Some come in plastic eggshells;
commercial embryos.

The contortions she goes through
to smooth her legs like silk,
wrestling these tubes
as her grandmother wrestled a corset;
bone-stiffened corset, ribbed
with the mouth parts of baleen whales.

Prescripted unnatural fibers
of viscous chemical milk,
strong and similar to
steel-belted radial tires;
market-wise; programmed, of course,
to self-destruct, unknit, ravel.

EMPATHY AGAIN

Have you considered the suffering of amoebas?
How the great rocks from the Oort Belt
threaten their fragile skins?
How, when they stretch their basic
and heroic pseudopods, salts,
which accumulate on almost all surfaces,
salts, which are ubiquitous hexagons,
crystals without caution or cognizance
and forming recklessly at random,
can slit the defenseless amoeba,
that single-celled miracle of chaos,
so that its magnificent improbable fluids
ooze; its remarkable self-propelled entity,
in the annals of unrecorded tragic events, deflates,
dehydrates, disappears; as though it never was.

BOOM

And the rock and rollers on the beach
crash into my, then, middle-aged shocked skull.
The TV ad swarms with the surfers cracking out the Coke—
plastic oil-glistened models in super film.
My Aunt Maud was addicted when it was real,
down in the smeared-over violent South.
Kept those original bottles in her non-electric ice box.
We weren't allowed to touch it. But we did.
I also sneaked into her homemade wine.
Hung over for a week in a feather bed,
I floated between her hawk-like face
and Uncle Cal's Southern-male nickering.
Baby Boomers, you're out there, those of you who lived,
fashioned for the products of this real world.
The same old shell game even the Egyptians
and the Sumerians knew. Now you're old,
as I was then, caught in these deadly traps
and what you bred. Your sperm fell
from the bombers overhead.
Greed in the spoiled contaminated waters
exploded like fatal fungus. And digital language
ate it like manna in the wilderness.

MOVING RIGHT ALONG

Advanced systems
came in the nineties,
with loss of conscience,
inability to feel. Sensation
was from then on secondhand.
Into this viscous spoil
I walked, perceiving faraway
lawns of deteriorating grasses,
sick trees, carefully separated
trash, the air steaming
with sewage.

Every detail, brilliant,
super enlarged, screaming
with dismemberment, ripped
sensations, debased dialogue;

time going faster
and faster, the collapse
of the initial bang
rushing into a thick goo
of bodies without separation;
as oil-slick,
as stripped molecules;
the sludge of hypothesis,
the word become flesh.

A LITTLE CHART

Unless and *more or less*
and *useless;*
that family of time
frittered away.
Let's say,
the sum of yesterday.
And *when* and *wherever*
and *whomsoever,*
gave its weight; its
actual avoirdupois,
the sliding scale
just tapped by the index finger
of the male nurse
but after you removed your shoes,
your polyfiber jacket
and put down your ten-pound purse.
And then, consider this . . .
breath is not weightless
nor is *therefore,*
thereupon, and *there . . .*
leading to the cage,
the ribs, the clavicle, the snare;
and then,
howsoever, howbeit, and
how come.
Which brings us back
full circle to—
I have ten fingers
but I am all thumb.

PRAYER OF DESCENDING ORDER

In Binghamton I wait to shed my hair.
Days are so thin. Radiation
splitting the conifers.
Snow, paranormal;
crystals isotopic, inferring
slippage. My feet thick with calluses,
the slag, the centuries of counterspin.

You who lie within,
between each word,
the space between the letters
of each word,
between the phonemes on the tongue,
between the tongue and teeth,
between the throat and palate;
you who leapt
from flesh to flesh;
you who chew the air
ravenous for my breath.

Mites, horned invisibles; cattle
or lizards of polyfiber rugs,
behemoths, dandruff eaters, consumers
of skin flakes; blessed monsters of the subworld.
Christ's children of my blindness, my unseen
holy mothers washing the dead. Cleansers
who also shit, are also cleaned, also
in angelic choirs descending, made pure
by those less and less, consuming nothing.
In their desire, praise emptiness, spirit.

ABOUT THE AUTHOR

Ruth Stone was born in 1915 in Roanoke,
Virginia. Her numerous honors include the Cerf
Lifetime Achievement Award from the state of
Vermont, the Whiting Award, the Bunting
Fellowship, two Guggenheim Fellowships, the
Delmore Schwartz Award, and the Shelley
Memorial Award. Ruth Stone is Professor of
English at the State University of New York,
Binghamton. She lives in Vermont.

ABOUT PARIS PRESS

Paris Press is a young nonprofit press publishing the work of women writers who have been neglected or misrepresented by the literary world. Publishing one to two books a year, Paris Press values work that is daring in style and in its courage to speak truthfully about society, culture, history, and the human heart. To publish our books, Paris Press relies on generous support from organizations and individuals. Please help Paris Press keep the voices of essential women writers in print and known. All contributions are tax-deductible.

The text of this book is composed in Joanna.
This typeface was designed in 1930 by
Eric Gill, who named it for his daughter.
Cover design by Judythe Sieck.
Text design by Ivan Holmes Design.
Composition by Potter Publishing Studio.
Drawing on cover by Siena Sanderson, b. 1956,
untitled pastel on paper, 30" x 22", 1993.
Siena Sanderson lives in New Mexico.
Photograph of Ruth Stone on back cover
by Jan Freeman.